YOU'VE

GW00777404

GOT

THIS!

YOU'VE

POWER

GOT

WITHIN

THIS!

AMANDA WILSON

You've Got This! Power Within
First published in Great Britain in 2018
Swirls Publishing Ltd

The moral right of the author has been asserted
ISBN 978 1 9996716 2 4 (paperback)
ISBN 978 1 9996716 3 1 (ebook)

www.swirlspublishing.co.uk

Amablices

For each
and
every one
of us

Life is supposed to be joyful
and for our deepest benefit.

Sometimes the biggest lessons
are in the struggle to unleash
the power within.

PREFACE

You've Got This! Power Within is intended to be a pick-me-up, a reminder, an injection shot to shift attitudes in that moment when we want and need to feel better about ourselves and what is going on in our lives.

It's an appetiser, an overview — made simple to whet your appetite for bringing about the change that you need so you can know and believe that — You've Got this! And — to rediscover the power that is within each and every one of us.

THE PROBLEM

Our inner power has become silenced by the loudness of the external. We have either forgotten the power that we have or, if we are aware of it, we tend to give it away. We never really knew, or we've forgotten how, to draw upon our power to create the lives we want. We react to the external as opposed to intentionally steering our lives in the direction we want to go in.

We don't have time. Life is busy enough without having to think about taking the time to fit something else into our already busy day.

Oh — if only we knew the irony!

THE SOLUTION

You've got the power! The journey to rediscovering our power will remind us that everything we need to be the powerhouse that we truly are lies within each and every one of us. Understanding how, as energetic beings, we are interacting with all energy in the Universe and that there are tools that we can use and practice regularly — this is how we claim back our power within.

WHAT IF

What if we had more control over our lives? Control to create the lives that we want, govern how we respond to people and situations and the experiences that present themselves to us; the good and the bad. What if we had the ability to achieve this without complete reliance on the outside world in order to feel better about ourselves? Imagine feeling good, right now and at any time, without having to wait for circumstances to be perfect and exactly how we want them to be.

Imagine ... we are in that space between where we are right now and where we want to be, we set the intention and work towards the goal, but we have tools so that we can be in that space and still feel good. How good would that be?

Over time, the focus has been towards the outside, the external — what is going on in the world around us, and this has quietened our inner guidance system. Our 'gut', our 'instinct', is a powerful intelligence guidance system that focuses on our best interest and steers us towards the best outcome for us.

What if we used tools to help us to connect with this guidance system again, knowing that in doing so, we can move to where we want to be, feeling empowered as we travel? We are the captains of our own ships and all that we need is available within us at any time to create the lives that we want and feel the joy we are aching to feel.

By connecting with the power within us, we can step into our own power, support ourselves and live our truth. We know deep down it's our right, but somehow along the way we have forgotten this; so we are going to rediscover and remind ourselves that we can determine how we feel, what experiences we have and that we have totally got this!

WATCH OUT!

Personal growth and changing how we move around in the world and with those around us, does come with a warning. It can be uncomfortable, unfamiliar and scary. Fear can take a hold so much so that the old patterns which aren't serving us seem so much more preferable than moving in to the discomfort zone. We know that we should 'feel the fear and do it anyway'. We know that outside of our comfort zones is where the magic happens. We know it; but doing something about it — wow, that takes strength and determination.

Then, if we are brave enough, we've got

to deal with the reactions of people around us who may not like the new version of ourselves — how we are taking control of our lives, investing in ourselves and reconnecting with our power within. Shaking off limiting beliefs and standing in our truth when someone else doesn't want to hear it or we fear they won't respond well isn't easy — this stuff is scary! But on the other side of believing in and supporting ourselves is freedom and confidence in ourselves and learning to trust our choices and the decisions we make. Freedom in practicing and then, with time, knowing, that whatever situation, person or experience is thrown at us, we will be okay. It's then your life opens up to who you really are and what you can become.

Taking back control of our lives and knowing we can do this is the most freeing and liberating gift we can give ourselves and other people around us. If we are at our happiest and a beacon of light, we shine that on those around us, right?

OUR PLACE IN
THE COSMOS

We are energy. Every miraculous bodily part and function is energy moving in and responding to the invisible Laws of the Universe and its laws of physics. How we interact with the world energetically influences what we experience — always. Once we understand this, we are empowered to break down any limiting beliefs and step into a new experience where anything really is possible.

The Universal Laws and the laws of physics are important if we are to understand why we experience what we do. Once we know this, we are empowered with knowledge and can start to do something about changing anything that doesn't work well for us. Our space in the cosmos and how we interact energetically within it is powerful. But we hold power, too; we have the power to influence our experience within it.

Are you ready to take back the control of your life — to feel empowered, connected to the cosmos and the forces within it and steer your life in the direction you want to go in? If you are, buckle up … you may never be the same again.

So, we know that we are energy and that everything around us in physical form is essentially energy — fact. Whether low or high energy (vibration), it is the energetic form of anything in the Universe — it is not judged, it just is. The Universal Law of Attraction describes how energetic forms respond to each other, in that like attracts like, and that which is like unto itself is drawn — like magnets. If our energy is vibrating at a low frequency, we will be tuned in to other low energy frequencies — which will show itself by the people we encounter and the experiences we have. This is without exception and judgement — every time; always.

Understanding the laws of physics is power. If we know how the world around us, which we can't see, operates, we can begin to learn about the tools we have available to us to change our energetic level so that we vibrate at a higher frequency and draw into our lives better-feeling experiences and people and improve the overall quality of our lives. Did you know you had this power?

How we manage our own energy before it goes out into the Universe is something that we *can* control; improving our mood, our energy and how we feel at any time. Just as laws govern our lives to provide stability, a framework in which we live, reduce chaos and uncertainty, the Law of Attraction is a Universal Law that can serve us to improve our lives.

Today, our lives are busier and faster than ever before. We are plugged in to technology to take us to other worlds, places and information

— quickly. But the speed at which we live in our lives can come at a price, that of disconnection from each other and ourselves.

We are a nation of doers, striving for success to get things done. We believe to achieve this requires action, and lots of it. The bigger the want, the harder we have to work to get it. We work hard for what we want and we work harder at pushing against that which we don't want, expelling every bit of energy we have, sometimes at the expense of our health and well-being.

What if getting what we want doesn't have to involve struggle? Hard work — yes, the hustle — yes, but not the relentless struggle. What if there was another way to deliberately create the wonderful lives we want? What could life be like then? What if we stopped looked outwardly as much to our external world, but started to look away from the fear, the scarcity we may feel and began to look within — to see who we really are the other side of fear and worry?

What if we became aware of our thoughts and how they benefit us, our feelings and how that

influences us, and build into our lives practices
to help us feel good?

WHAT
DO YOU THINK?

Our thoughts are more powerful than we know. They are the signals sent out to the cosmos, the Universe. So, whatever the thought is that is being sent out, it directly influences how we are feeling and how we are vibrating energetically. We will attract back to us, every time, that which is like itself. So, if we feel good because we are thinking good-feeling thoughts, we attract more 'like' experiences back to us. We're magnetising more of the same. And, because the Law of Attraction does not judge, filter or advise, if we think negative thoughts and put their energy out there into the ether, the signal will attract the same 'like' experiences of that vibration back to us.

For many of us, moving through life, feeling like we have no control over how life events may unravel, the default position is, 'I'm fine' — without us realising what we are magnetising back to us in our future; that is, more feeling 'just alright'. We feel like we are observers to what is shown to us or thrown at us in life and we feel out of control. But what if we could take back the control, intentionally think good thoughts to attract like energy, experiences, events and people into our lives? Remind yourself of your dreams, goals and aspirations. How empowering could this be? We could move from feeling OK and alright, to good — even fantastic — most of the time. Or, even if we don't feel great, we begin to understand why it is we don't and we can start to do something about it.

Then it's our feelings. How do you feel? Now we know the power of our thoughts in directly influencing how we feel and how we vibrate, in drawing back like experiences into our reality to match our vibration, how we feel becomes our guidance system. If we're not feeling great, we're not thinking thoughts to make us feel great. So, change the thought to change how you feel. If we are radiating joy and feeling in balance and in harmony with our lot, well, great — we will be pulling more of the very same in to fuel that happiness.

For some, taking the time to reflect on how you feel may be new and uncomfortable. Most of us are busy working (with the support of loving mentors and colleagues, or not) some of us are raising families (with the support of a loving partner, or not) and navigating our way through our lives as best we can, with what we know. Most of the time we pay little attention to how we feel, ignoring the fact that we don't feel great, and we carry on regardless. This sets the wheels in motion for us to receive more of the same not-so-great experiences, and on and on it goes, into our future.

This makes us react in different ways.

Some may take action to numb the pain and pretend it isn't there. Some respond to this disempowerment by venting frustration at others, reacting to external circumstances that feel beyond their control. At best, we may feel OK most of the time, with just moments of joy scattered every now and then to remind us what we are missing. But how we feel can help us.

How we feel is our guide to what thoughts we are thinking. How we are feeling is our connecting mechanism with the Universal Law of Attraction. Our vibration is the communication system with the Universe, the Universal Law of Attraction and the physical manifestation of what comes into our lives. Everything you have vibrated up until now, every thought and feeling experienced, has brought into reality a like match to your energy and how you have been vibrating and what you have been asking for — without even knowing it! The good news is we can change this at any time. How do we do this? It's simple — find ways to be happy now.

RIGHT HERE, RIGHT NOW

All of our power is in this moment, right now. We can dwell on the past as much as we want or convince ourselves that as soon as we get the promotion, the job, the loving relationship, then we'll be happy. If we think like this, happiness is always out of our reach — it's in the future and somehow unobtainable, though we know we want it now. So, before you embrace the power of the moment to be happy, first you must allow yourself to be happy.

We are all worthy of having great lives, being everything we want to be, and not settling for less. The Universe is abundant with infinite possibilities and is working for our benefit — imagine that! But it's often our limiting perception of what is or isn't possible that stops us from embracing happiness, keeping it away from us, always over there. You don't have to wait for external circumstances to be right before you can be happy. Be happy now and you increase your chance of having what it is you are wanting, by creating the power in the moment, feeling good and vibrating what you want back to you.

Intentionally create your life by guiding thoughts to a better-feeling place, sending out the signal and vibrations to the Universe to manifest the results of the good vibrations into our lives. And when we are thinking good thoughts, feeling good and sending our vibrations to magnetise like experiences back into our physical world, this is when we can start intentionally creating the lives we want and practice manifesting our desires into our lives. Everything — the parking space right outside the shop, a great relationship, money flowing abundantly, a job that satisfies, nurtures our skills and rewards us, neighbours who are respectful, to feeling at peace with ourselves — can be ours.

CREATE THE LIFE
YOU WANT

What is it you want?

Before we can deliberately create our lives by the vibrations that we offer out, we must begin by knowing what it is we want. This sounds simple enough, but rediscovering what it is we truly want in life, what makes us feel on top of the world and like we are living our best life, can take some time to achieve.

The default setting that many of us have lived, or are living our lives by, have us observing and reacting to the world around us, without actively focusing on what it is we really want. We get drawn in to situations we don't want to be in, dramas that are playing out in front of us, and we react to life. Deep down, where the child in us is full of hope that anything is possible, this is where you can make a start, by reconnecting with yourself. What is it that you want? Then supersize it and dream really big. One thing is for sure, you will never achieve your goals if you don't know what they are and you don't bring them to life again and into your everyday experience, in the form of reminding yourself what they are.

Dream big, imagine you are at your best, when you could be, do and have anything you want and, in that moment whilst you are reconnecting with your true wants, put self-doubt, the inner critic and all self-defining limitations aside. As part of this practice, it will be as important to identify what it is you don't want. So, embrace any don't wants that may pop up as part of the process, too. We know what hasn't worked for us in the past, so listen to that inner guidance. It is important to know that there is no right or wrong way to do this, and — You've Got This!

Be clear on what you want and set goals that move you towards achieving it.

The asking we are talking about here is full-bodied asking, where we feel what we want to the point that it feels real in our experience. Move beyond wanting (though this is where a lot of us can get stuck) and we feel like we have it now, so much so that we attract it into existence. But you really have to feel this. Feel the joy of a new relationship, the support, and the loving arms wrapped around you, as if it were happening now.

This requires imagination and faith. Don't worry about *how* this is going to happen, that's not your job. Let the Universe, with the infinite possibilities it has available, take care of the *how*.

Then, allow it to happen

The third practice is to allow the space between what it is you want and receiving it. Asking again and again suggests a lack of belief that it will be delivered, so it probably won't be. This does require trust that it will happen and letting go of the outcome. Notice what is coming into your experience which may lead you to what it is you have asked for. Allow yourself to be happy. Fear of being happy, because if we feel too good it may be all pulled away from under us, is what can hold us apart from truly feeling what it is we want. Make the decision to be happy now.

POWER WITHIN
DAILY PRACTICES

There are many ways we can begin to feel better about ourselves. When you follow these practices regularly, you will start to feel better and see results. We cannot change others, but we can change ourselves and how we respond to others, and be the change we want to see in the world. Bring each practice into your life gradually and form a morning routine that suits you, made up of a few of these that resonate with you the most.

When you take the time, every day, to start you day in this way you are setting yourself up, shifting your attitude to a better state of mind, grounding yourself for what lies ahead and reminding yourself of the bigger picture — that is, who you are and what you want to do and be, and that you are working towards all of it. Our morning routine is one of *the* best ways to intentionally use the power we have to create the lives we want.

GRATITUDE

Practicing gratitude is powerful; it can shift a bad-feeling state in an instant. When we are thankful for what we have right now, even if we don't have everything we want, we are sending a signal of appreciation out to the cosmos, to the Universe — allowing better-feeling experiences to come to us. The shift in perspective in remembering reasons to be grateful can lift a mood instantly, make us feel better, raise our energy levels to a more positive-feeling, lighter state and set us up to attract more of the same, like for like experiences towards us.

Morning bursts of gratitude will set you up

for the day. Think of three things that you are grateful for. Really think about each one. How does it make you feel? What are the benefits to you? A child's health, supportive family, doing a job you love, your comfy slippers. Big or small — anything counts.

Practice this every day for a week and notice how your mood changes. Regular practice will change the way you look at things; you may well start to look for the good in a situation.

When we start to believe something, we start to see evidence of it. So be grateful and start to see evidence of more things to be grateful for. Start to feel good about what you do have and avoid focusing on the lack and what hasn't come to you yet. This is the journey to feeling better immediately and changing our state to harness our power within.

QUIET

The power within us is louder when we quieten our minds and are still for a while. In the stillness we hear and feel the essence of who we are and the power inside us. In the stillness we are connected with the hope and joy of the cosmos, of the Universe — the truth of who we are. In stillness and quiet, we can let go of worry, anxiety and fear, since they don't need to be heard all the time.

Mindfulness or meditation can be sitting quietly for at least five minutes as we listen to our breathing, or taking a walk in nature, where we may feel the same connection with the life force around us. However we prefer to achieve quiet, when we do, our chattering minds will quieten down. There comes a stillness and peace where worry and fear lose their power and our own strength can be felt and heard. In the absence of noise and interaction, you'll discover that there is so much.

Sit quietly now, somewhere comfortable, and be still. As thoughts rise up and we start to engage with answering them, or concerning ourselves with how we resolve the thought, let them just be. Let them pass by — neither to be resolved nor understood. There is no call to action other than to recognise its presence of being and let it go. Come back to the quiet.

One of the most effective clearing of the mind exercises is journaling. Journaling is best done in the morning. Take an A4 pad and pen and write three pages of your thoughts. Write anything and everything that comes to you. The chatter, the worries, the things we have to do (I also write those in the margin, which forms part of my to-do list for the day). Journaling releases, counsels, and is a facilitator of change. It awakens our thoughts, worries and power and becomes our ally in getting everything out on the pages and clearing our way.

Journaling — or 'Morning Pages', as Julia Cameron describes it in *The Artist's Way* — is one of the basic tools for creative recovery, allowing us to reconnect with our creative selves. These need not be edited; they're written for your eyes only and not to be re-read immediately. They are a clearing ground so that we can get beyond the noise — get the worries, fears and anxieties down on paper, exposed, talked about so that we can start to see beyond them — see that we are not at the mercy of our chattering mind and we can, in fact, control how powerful it is or isn't to us. In the clearing we rediscover our true and stronger sense of self.

KEEP
GOOD COMPANY

Who and what we surround ourselves with has a big impact, so keep good company as much as you can. Reading a passage in a book or content on social media can serve as a good pick-me-up and attitude-shifter. The power of one sentence to change the way we think and feel in a moment should not be underestimated. So be part of groups and add people to your platforms whose energy and passion and hunger for nurturing your power within will support you.

Look for people who you aspire to be like; they

are evidence that this is possible. Similarly, be aware of negativity and your exposure. We are all responsible to be aware of and take action for what is going on in the world, but bombarding yourself with news of doom and gloom can lead to a state of hopelessness — so keep good company in the content that you expose yourself to.

This includes the people we surround ourselves with. For those who we have direct control over how much we expose ourselves to, make sure you surround yourself with people who support you and your dreams. Not everyone will be on the same journey as we are. Audit your circle. Limit exposure to family or friends who don't make you feel good about yourself. Have the uncomfortable conversation to support yourself and make it known if 'that doesn't work for me', or say 'Can you not say/do that in my company, please,' when people aren't, intentionally or not, respecting your wants and needs.

By supporting ourselves we step into our power and represent ourselves. Said kindly, yet firmly, we are empowered to voice our boundaries and state what is and isn't acceptable to us. This does come with a word of caution — that a change in behaviour will trigger some people to really test our resolve. These are our biggest teachers. Keep strong, they will adjust, they have no choice but to do so. If they don't and their company no longer serves you, parting ways is sometimes the biggest gift we can give ourselves. Relationships should be respectful and kind, not a battlefield and a transaction for gain; if they are, these are areas to work on improving and if it doesn't work — then let them go.

Surround yourself with winners in your field. Find evidence of success and examples of what it is we are striving for. Hunger and confidence is contagious. You will feed off it.

Beware of negative or toxic people around you and limit your exposure to them as much as possible. This may be difficult if it's a family member or work colleague, but there are ways of communicating whilst keeping a wide berth, ways of dealing on your own terms and without being pulled into their drama. It's their drama and their business, so let them get on with it — you get on with keeping your distance. Remember, keep those feel-good feelings in focus and don't make it your business to fix something or someone else; they are responsible for their own experience.

SET
BOUNDARIES

This is a tough one — but when mastered, this is a game changer. Self-care is not selfish. It is fundamental to wholesome and wholehearted relationships. When we know ourselves, respect ourselves and have clear boundaries in place, we can navigate through the world fearlessly, knowing that we have the tools and the power to get through anything.

Putting other people before you to your own detriment and prioritising a constant compulsion to people-please over your own needs and wants, is a guarantee that we will feel that our tank is empty — we are constantly giving out to others and no one is respecting what we want, because we don't have boundaries clearly defined for others to respect. This can manifest in over-giving in relationships and receiving little back, becoming resentful and losing our power. 'Love thy neighbour as you love yourself,' tells us to love ourselves first — then love others.

BE YOUR OWN CHEERLEADER

When life gets too crazy and you feel overwhelmed, put the brakes on. There are times when life is so frantic that we forget to look after ourselves, let alone remember and have time to practice techniques to make us feel better — life is busy enough! When this happens to me, I visualise pushing down that brake pedal and slowing down, even stopping, sometimes. Being mindful of this process allows you to operate better in the busy times. Don't push or exhaust yourself, you don't have to. Put the brake on now and again, take stock and recharge, to give you the bump start needed.

Be your own best friend. Allow yourself to rest, exercise and do one nice thing for yourself every day (little gestures count). When we are self-respecting we set the boundaries for how we expect others to treat us. Be nice to others, it will make them feel good and be nice back. Monitor the self-talk and the criticism which may be playing in your mind on repeat. It really isn't helping or true, but it's still playing the same old story unchallenged.

FOCUS ON WHAT
YOU WANT

Once you have reminded yourself what it is you want to be, do and have, make it part of your every day. Two powerful tools to use are affirmations and visualisation. Affirmations are a powerful tool; using them, we reaffirm regularly (daily, if possible) what it is we want to do, be and have, using simple statements, setting our intention that:

I am a successful author.

I am teaching children all over the world that we hold the power to achieve anything we want.

I am loved.

And the big one …

I am enough.

These statements remind us of our power. Say it to yourself, say it out loud or say it in front of the mirror. Say it, over and over again. Make it one of the first things that you do in the morning before you start your day.

Visualisation is a way of bringing our visions to life of what it is we want to be, do and have. It moves us beyond where we are and reminds us of our dreams, our goals and aspirations; the things we have forgotten along the way, when life gets busy, our responsibilities change and we stop thinking about what really does light our fire. Remember your dreams and aspirations and bring them to life on a vision board. Look at these images every day and imagine that you are in that scene of the holiday on the boat, laughing, with your family around you, or moving to the city or the town you have pinned to your vision board.

These tools are powerful. They support your

belief. Surround yourself with what it is you want your future to look like — imagine it, look at it, bring it into your reality and your focus, moving towards it in the goals you set. Setting goals and proactively taking action towards what it is you want to achieve will build momentum in moving towards what you want.

TRUST
YOUR INSTINCTS

Our instincts are our guide. They have our best intentions at heart and are privy to information beyond that which we can see, hear or know. Living in the Age of Distraction, our reliance and value on action and doing have muted our instincts. By sitting quietly for only a few minutes every day we can reconnect with our inner radar, which exists to navigate us through our best life. So, take notice of feelings that feel right or wrong, our instincts are guiding us every time. When you really learn to listen and trust your instincts, decisions based on how something feels become effortless and you will cease living out the result of a choice that never felt right in the first place.

Fear of making the wrong decision can be paralysing. To move beyond the fear, acknowledge that making the wrong decision is part of life, or having a situation turn out differently than we expected is part of life, but at any time we can make the decision to make a change. Sometimes it's not until much later that you'll understand the benefits of the decision you made.

When something doesn't feel right, it's often a no. Sometimes, when something doesn't feel right, it's our fear getting in the way. So there's some working out to do to see which one is which, but in the meantime, know there is no bad decision and you can make a change. Considered decisions are important. Paralysis in making a decision — not so much. You've got this, you'll be OK whatever you decide to do, because you have your power within to call on at any time.

ASK
FOR HELP

Asking for help of any kind is not a weakness. Knowing when we need help from friends, a teacher, parents — anyone — that is a strength. Besides, we cannot survive alone; we are social creatures, meant to interact and connect with others. People are often only too glad to help.

Professional help, in the form of a life coach or therapist, can be life-changing and the best gift we can give ourselves to move beyond a place where we may feel stuck and to experience the shift we need to let in the change.

OUR BODY

Our bodies are the vehicle in which we move around and exist in the world we live in. A well-nourished, rested, physically active body will assist us in being our best selves. The release of endorphins when we exercise makes us feel better. When we look after our bodies with what we eat, making sure we nurture it with the vitamins and minerals it needs, we feel better. Resting after we push ourselves, taking notice when our bodies tell us something through what we are feeling in it, is essential.

Our body is ours to take care of, to take charge of and promote our best feeling, energy flowing, high vibrations. A blocked, undernourished body will not promote good feeling, so get moving, get outside and be in nature for the restorative and calming effects that has on us. Take a run, a long walk, weed the garden ... whatever it is, just get out. When you look after your body, you will feel self-respecting and strong.

IT'S NOT
WORKING...

So, what if it's not happening fast enough, or at all? What if everything we have been wanting and feeling is not coming into physical form? One of the most common reasons is because we are focusing on what we don't want or focusing on the absence of what we do want. It's a subtle difference in the emphasis on focus, but powerful enough to resonate out to the Universe to magnetise like experiences back to us every time — more not having and more wanting.

Do check in with yourself to see where your

focus is. A subtle change to the feeling of already having and how wonderful it is to have it in your life already and how much gratitude you have for having it, thank you very much, is all you need.

KEEP GOING

So, what if we're looking after our physical bodies, exercising so that we expend energy, balance and strengthen our bodies, we're practicing meditation or have short bursts of time where we can stop and calm our minds, but we still have moments, or days — or even longer stretches of time — where we just can't improve how we feel. And, worse still, now we know how the Law of Attraction works, this makes us feel even more frustrated, knowing we are attracting back more of the not feeling so good experiences back to us. Just keep on keeping on with the techniques and practice set out here. It's like a finely honed muscle, you'll only get better at using it, so don't be too hard on yourself.

ABOUT THE AUTHOR

Amanda Wilson lives in Surrey, England. With a Bachelor of Arts Humanities degree, majoring in European literature, she has a passion for storytelling and its power to transform the way that we think and feel about our place in the world. Amanda has enjoyed a twenty-year career in broadcasting, with writing and researching into personal development prominent in her personal life. Amanda writes children's fiction (*Tubular Swirls — The Call to Angels* is the first book in the *Tubular Swirls* trilogy) and creates children's picture books.

EVEN IN THE DARKEST SKY,
RAINBOWS ARE POSSIBLE.

TUBULAR
SWIRLS
The Call to Angels

Amanda Wilson

EARTH IS IN TROUBLE

A fallen angel has taken the Seventh Sphere and Mickey and his friends from the Angel Academy embark on a mission to find it. Meanwhile Zachary Blake and his gang are on a mission to stop them at any cost. When Mickey is attacked by Blake and his thugs, his wings are injured. In his despair he discovers the Power 5 and learns that the greatest power lies within ourselves.

Will Mickey find the inner strength to fly again and will the Sphere ever be found?

Tubular Swirls — The Call to Angels,
the first book in the *Tubular Swirls* trilogy,
is available as Kindle e-book and paperback
on Amazon.co.uk and Amazon.com

COMING SOON

If you would like to find out any more
about the titles available or coming soon,
please view our website
swirlspublishing.co.uk

To receive updates about new books, early chapter
reads and giveaways - sign up to our newsletter at
books@swirlspublishing.co.uk

NOTES

NOTES

NOTES

NOTES

40872275R00047

Printed in Poland
by Amazon Fulfillment
Poland Sp. z o.o., Wrocław